HAIL!
TUDORS

Philip Steele

Crabtree Publishing Company

www.crabtreebooks.com

Crabtree Publishing Company

www.crabtreebooks.com

Author: Philip Steele
Editor: Lynn Peppas
Project coordinator: Kathy Middleton
Production coordinator: Ken Wright
Prepress technician: Ken Wright
Managing editor: Miranda Smith
Designer: Lorna Phillips
Picture researcher: Clare Newman
Design manager: David Poole
Editorial director: Lindsey Lowe
Children's publisher: Anne O'Daly
Consultant: Dr Paul G. Bahn

Photographs:
Bridgeman Art Library: Historic New England,
   Boston, Massachusetts, USA: p. 21 (bottom right)
Getty Images: Creativ Studio Heinemann: p. 12 (eel),
   Dorling Kindersley: p. 12 (hare)
iStockphoto: Sean Curry: p. 15 (bottom right);
   Natalia Galkina: p. 21 (bottom left); Hulton
   Archives: p. 15 (bottom left); Rmax: p. 17
   (center left); Duncan Walker: p. 6 (left), 10 (center
   left), 10 (center right), 11 (top left), 11 (bottom left),
   14 (center); Steven Wynn: p. 26 (center right)

Mary Evans Picture Library: p. 4
Photolibrary: The National Trust Photo Library:
   p. 20 (bottom right top), 21 (top right top)
Thinkstock: p. 3 (top right), 3 (bottom center),
   5 (bottom right), 6 (center right), 7 (center left),
   7 (top left and right), 8 (center left), 8 (center right),
   9 (bottom right), 18 (bottom left), 19 (center
   bottom), 19 (bottom left), 27 (top center), 29 (center
   right)
Topham: p. 5 (bottom left), 11 (top and bottom right),
   16 (top left), 20 (top right), 21 (top left), 26 (bottom
   right), 28 (center); Artmedia/HIP: p. 15 (bottom
   right); Roger-Viollet: p. 9 (top left), 19 (center
   right), 29 (center left); The Granger Collection:
   p. 25 (bottom right), 26 (top left); The Print
   Collector/HIP: p. 7 (center); UK City Images:
   p. 20 (bottom right); Woodmansterne: p. 13
   (bottom)
Andrew Webb: p. 10-11 (background)
Wikimedia: p. 7 (bottom right)
Other images by Shutterstock

This book was produced for Crabtree Publishing
Company by Brown Reference Group.

Library and Archives Canada Cataloguing in Publication

Steele, Philip, 1948-
      Hail! Tudors / Philip Steele.

(Hail! History)
Includes index.
ISBN 978-0-7787-6626-1 (bound).--ISBN 978-0-7787-6633-9 (pbk.)

      1. Tudor, House of--Juvenile literature. 2. Great Britain--Social
life and customs--16th century--Juvenile literature. 3. Great
Britain--History--Tudors, 1485-1603--Juvenile literature. I. Title.
II. Title: Tudors. III. Series: Hail! History

DA315.S74 2010   j942.05   C2010-901290-9

Library of Congress Cataloging-in-Publication Data

Steele, Philip, 1948-
  Hail! Tudors / Philip Steele.
      p. cm. -- (Hail! History)
  Includes index.
  ISBN 978-0-7787-6626-1 (reinforced library binding : alk. paper) --
ISBN 978-0-7787-6633-9 (pbk. : alk. paper)
  1. Tudor, House of--Juvenile literature. 2. Great Britain--Social life
and customs--16th century--Juvenile literature. 3. Great Britain--
History--Tudors, 1485-1603--Juvenile literature. I. Title. II. Title:
Tudors. III. Series.

  DA315.S74 2010
  942.05--dc22
                                                2010006630

Crabtree Publishing Company
www.crabtreebooks.com   1-800-387-7650

Printed in Hong Kong/042011/BK20110304

Published in Canada
Crabtree Publishing
616 Welland Ave.
St. Catharines, Ontario
L2M 5V6

Published in the United States
Crabtree Publishing
PMB 59051
350 Fifth Avenue, 59th Floor
New York, New York 10118

CONTENTS

THE TUDORS

Let us sound a fanfare for the Tudors, the royal family who changed the history of the British Isles between 1485 and 1603 CE. *HAIL!* sent their journalists to take the pulse of those stormy times. Read their cutting-edge articles about Tudor attitudes to fashion, scandal, fame, and power. It is a great story—but were the Tudors marvels or monsters?

LOOKING BACK

The Tudors first ruled over England, Wales, and Ireland during the final years of the Middle Ages. When their rule ended, the modern world was taking shape. The story of the Tudors starts here...

THE FIRST TUDOR MONARCH

England was torn apart by the Wars of the Roses that began around 1455 CE. Two rival dynasties, York and Lancaster, fought for the throne. In 1485, the exiled Henry Tudor, 2nd Earl of Richmond, landed in Wales. Henry's army defeated and killed Richard III at Bosworth field, and he was crowned Henry VII, the first ruler of the Tudor dynasty.

Henry VII

TUDOR DYNASTY

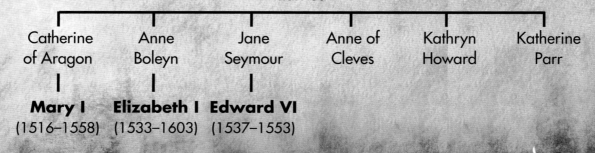

Henry VII   married   Elizabeth of York
(1457–1509)

Henry VIII
(1491–1547)

married

Catherine of Aragon	Anne Boleyn	Jane Seymour	Anne of Cleves	Kathryn Howard	Katherine Parr
Mary I (1516–1558)	Elizabeth I (1533–1603)	Edward VI (1537–1553)			

HAIL! QUIZ WHAT MADE THE TUDORS TICK?

Enter our readers' poll and select your favorite from these five key achievements.

1. THEATER AND THE ARTS
The Tudor kings and queens were patrons of music, dance, literature, and the theater. The playwright William Shakespeare made his name during the reign of Elizabeth I. His plays would become famous around the world.

2. EXPLORATION
During the Tudor period, the explorer John Cabot sailed from Bristol, England, to reach Newfoundland in Canada, Martin Frobisher explored Canada, Francis Drake sailed around the world, and Sir Walter Raleigh attempted to found a colony in Virginia in North America. The world was opening up to travel and trade.

3. PALACES
Fine palaces were built in England during the Tudor period—Richmond, Hampton Court, Whitehall, and Nonesuch. They replaced the old stone castles and were beautfully furnished with tapestries and carved wood. These palaces provided the backdrop to the grand ceremonies and glittering celebrations of the royal court.

4. A GROWING POWER
England began to be rated as a major power in Europe. Henry VIII and later Elizabeth I built a royal navy. England became a serious rival to Spain, whose invading Armada was defeated in 1588.

5. TRADE AND WEALTH
Wool and woolen cloth were the biggest exports at the start of the Tudor period. Lead, tin, and coal mines were opened up and flourished. Ships sailed into the port of London from all over Europe. Treasure looted from Spanish ships in the New World ended up in England, too.

Submit Your Answer

Right Royals! pp. 10–11

SEE INSIDE:

Fashion Tips pp. 14–15

Stage people pp. 22–23

REGULAR CONTRIBUTORS: Henry VIII, Thomas Cromwell, Dr. John Dee, Walter Raleigh

HUNK OF THE MONTH
HENRY VIII

In his younger days, Henry was hot! At 6 feet 3 inches (190 cm), with a 36 inch (91 cm) waist, he caused quite a flutter among the ladies of the royal court. Henry was the sporty type, an ace at indoor tennis and a great gambler.

Kapow!

Another sport for fit young princes in the 1500s? Jousting! In a tournament, you sit on a horse and charge at your opponent in the arena, getting points for knocking him off his horse. Henry loves all this medieval stuff. In his suit of armor he was fashionably "dressed to kill!"

WHO ATE ALL THE PIES?

By the time of his death, at 55 years old, Henry VIII was not a pretty sight. He had little eyes in a fat face and his waist had ballooned to 55 inches (140 cm). He was covered in boils and it took four strong men to carry him. He probably died of diabetes brought on by his poor diet and extra weight.

▲ In his prime, Henry wore the finest clothes and cut a dashing figure.

HOW TO LOSE FRIENDS...

Easy, start chopping off their heads! A couple of days after his coronation, Henry had two ministers arrested and executed. Other celebs who got (literally) axed—Sir Thomas More (left), the Bishop of Rochester, Thomas Cromwell (right). The one thing Henry cannot stand is people who disagree with him. What is the point of being king if you can't get your own way?

SO, WOLSEY...

HAIL! interviewed top political adviser Cardinal Wolsey shortly before he died—on his way to be tried for treason.

"I could see things were getting bad between Henry and myself, so I gave him my palace at Hampton Court—state of the art, every modern convenience. And he said, 'Hey, thanks very much, but tough—you're finished anyway..' Well, it seems that he was right on that one."

Pop Idol!

This king of pop really is a king. Henry VIII is a monarch who just loves to dance. He collects musical instruments, from bagpipes to flutes and virginals, and employs 58 full-time musicians. He enjoys all sorts of sounds, from church and court music to popular love songs. He plays the lute (left) very well, and even writes his own songs.

Greatest Hits
- *Hélas Madame*
- *Pastime with Good Company*

French encounter

In 1514, Henry met the French king, François I, for 17 days of sporting combat. The meeting was intended to increase their "bond of friendship." Their camp was called the Field of the Cloth of Gold and it was near Calais in France. Each monarch tried to outdo the other—in gold, fancy fashions, flags, and pavilions. There were 2,800 tents, fountains running with red wine, and 2,200 sheep to be barbecued. It was the party of the century!

François Talks!

King François I of France speaks out

"So Henry and I decided to enter into the spirit of things and have a wrestling match. He was useless! And then he went all moody on everyone because I won. *Sacré bleu*, bad losers, *ces Anglais*!"

LONELY HEARTS

Henry was married six times. He changed the course of history by breaking from the Catholic Church to divorce his first wife, Catherine of Aragon, and marry Anne Boleyn.

No son, we're done!

EXCLUSIVE: Catherine Speaks

" Not only is Henry dumping me for a younger woman, he's saying we were never properly married in the first place. And all because my first husband was his brother! Henry wants a divorce, but the Pope won't let him. **"**

HEADS WILL ROLL

" I have but a little neck "

Henry was desperate to marry Anne Boleyn. The Pope refused to annul Henry's marriage to Catherine, but Henry went ahead anyway. Anne and Henry married in 1533, when she was already pregnant with Elizabeth. The archbishop of Canterbury declared Henry's first marriage invalid and England broke from the Catholic Church. But Henry soon tired of Anne. She did not give him a male heir and became unpopular with the people. She was condemned for adultery and was beheaded in 1536.

Lovely, But Not Very Well

Jane Seymour caught Henry's eye in 1535. He was certainly keen. They got engaged within 24 hours of Anne Boleyn losing her head and married three weeks later. The marriage was happy but short. Their son and heir Edward was born in 1537. But Jane died just two weeks later.

Together forever—Jane was the only wife to be buried with Henry.

WHAT A MARE!

Anne of Cleves Hits Back!

"Henry says he fell in love with my picture but now he calls me the Flanders mare. What an insult! OK, so I'm no oil painting, but look at him? I'm not going to make a fuss. If he wants a divorce, he can have one. I've seen what happened to his other wives. I'll just take the money and the castles and keep quiet."

Before Henry...
- **Flemish aristocrat** available for strategic alliance. Easy-going with good sense of humor. Does not hunt, sing, or play a musical instrument. Only speaks German. Fairly attractive; pictures available.

As pretty as a picture?

Rose Without a Thorn

When they married in 1540, Kathryn Howard was 19 while Henry was 49, massive, and bloated with a lame leg. Henry was enchanted. He called her his "rose without a thorn" and showered her with gifts. But rumors spread about Kathryn's affairs, and she was executed in 1542.

Before Henry...
- **Young, attractive** woman with influential uncle seeks husband. Age no object.

DOMESTIC GODDESS

As someone who has been married twice before, to elderly husbands, Katherine Parr is ideal to become Henry's sixth wife. When Henry began to court Katherine, he had stiff competition in the dashing Sir Thomas Seymour. Henry cunningly arranged for Thomas to be sent as a special ambassador to Belgium and the wedding went ahead. It was a family affair with the king's children all in attendance.

Before Henry...
- **Twice widowed,** caring, good with children. Well educated and good at languages (fluent in French, Italian, and Latin).

THE HIT LIST

Catherine of Aragon
b.1485, d.1536
Divorced ✖

Anne Boleyn
b.1500?, d.1536
Beheaded 🪓

Jane Seymour
b.1509, d.1537
Died RIP

Anne of Cleves
b.1515, d.1557
Annulment ✖

Kathryn Howard
b.1521, d.1542
Beheaded 🪓

Katherine Parr
b.1512, d.1548
Survived ✔

RIGHT ROYALS!

Those Tudor monarchs really were a mixed bunch—the good, the bad, and the ugly! But they knew how to get themselves talked about. Henry and Elizabeth are in all the movies and TV shows hundreds of years later...

" The crown is rightly my right. "

Not a Well Boy

Edward VI took over as king in 1547. His dad was Henry VIII and his mom was wife number 3, Jane Seymour. Edward came to the throne when he was only nine years old. He was schooled as a Protestant and the serious business of ruling was left to nobles and relatives. Sadly, young Ed died in 1553, at the age of 15, probably of TB.

A Nine-day Wonder

When Edward VI was on his deathbed, he was persuaded to change his will so that his teenaged cousin Lady Jane Grey could become queen. She was another Protestant, a nice and extremely clever young girl, who was being bossed about by grown-ups who wanted power. She was crowned in 1553 but overthrown in just nine days, and some months later had her head cut off.

Did you know?

This was the shortest reign in English history.

> ## She was called Bloody Mary. "

> ## " I have the heart and stomach of a king. "

CONTRARY MARY

The second coronation in 1553 was for Mary I, daughter of Henry and wife number 1, Catherine of Aragon. Mary really was not a merry monarch. She did not like Anne Boleyn's daughter Elizabeth being around. Mary was Catholic and could not stand Protestants—even her half—sister Elizabeth. She had nearly 300 of them burned alive during her reign, which lasted five years, until her death in 1558.
p.s. Mary did like the Catholic king, Philip II of Spain—in fact she married him!

A Virgin Queen?

Mary had no kids, so the next in line is Princess Elizabeth. Flame-haired Bess loves dancing. She is a real linguist and has her head screwed on tight (which is just as well in these axe-happy days). She has what it takes and people love her for it. A real celeb, Elizabeth travels all around the country. She rarely misses a portrait op (provided it is flattering) and at court every eye is upon her. But she has a fierce temper, just like her dad!

So how did a King of Spain make out as King of England? *HAIL!* traveled to the land of oranges and castles to ask the man himself.

> OK, I admire the lady a lot. She's a good Catholic, but a little bit cranky, if you know what I mean? And she's getting on a bit. And the weather up there's not so sunny. *Dios mio, los Ingleses* are a little bit miserable, are they not? "

A Royal Wedding?
Will she, won't she?

Elizabeth has certainly liked to keep her admirers guessing! But is that just a smart political move? And now she says she will not marry anyone at all! But there are rumors that she and Robert Dudley are more than just good friends!

What's in your FRIDGE?

Tudors liked meat, and lots of it. It was roasted, boiled, and put into pies. Food could not be frozen so it was preserved or eaten fresh.

Did you know?

Sugar is a luxury and only for the rich. Most people use honey as a sweetener.

Meat
Hares, pigs, deer, calves, and wild boar are popular. All parts of the animal are eaten.

Birds
Swans, pheasants, herons, bitterns, partridges, quails, pigeons, larks, chickens, and sparrows are all on the menu.

Fish
Fish is eaten on Fridays and during Lent. Choose from eels, pike, salmon, whiting, haddock, bass, carp, crabs, lobster, porpoise, and seal.

Spices
Meat is salted or pickled to last longer. Spices such as pepper, nutmeg, and ginger are useful to disguise the salt and the taste of rotten meat.

Vegetables
Eaten in small amounts and only when in season.

Soup, soup, and more soup

Food for the poor is pottage (soup made of herbs) and bread.

BREAD BASKET

Bread is served at every meal. Poor people eat carter's bread. Made from rye and wheat, it is black or dark brown in color. Rich people eat a fine, white bread called manchet. In between is raveled bread, made from whole wheat flour with the bran left in.

Our nutritionist says:

- This is a typical Tudor diet, high in protein, fats, and sugars. Bad teeth and skin disease are common.
- Don't drink the water! Rich people drink wine, and everyone drinks ale.
- Dairy foods, fresh fruit, and root vegetables are eaten by the poor.

HOW TO THROW A DINNER PARTY

Feasts and banquets were lavish affairs with lots of dishes, the finest ingredients, and unusual recipes.

Menu

First Course
Brawn (boar meat)
Roast tongue
Leg of pork
Roast beef
Roast venison
Meat pie
Vegetables in season

Second Course
Roast lamb,
Rabbit, Bread

Dessert
Tarts and custard

Sheep's Feet

To make the best sheep's feet, take sheep's feet, slit the bone, and pick them very clean. Place in frying–pan, with a ladleful of strong broth and butter.

To impress guests, serve a cockatrice (the front of a rooster sewn to the back of a pig) or roasted peacock served in its own skin.

DOs AND DON'Ts

✔ Do wash your hands where everyone can see them. You'll be taking food from shared plates so people will want to see that your hands are clean.

✖ Don't put your fingers in your ears while you're eating, and don't blow your nose on your napkin.

✔ Do throw the bones on the floor when you've picked aff the meat.

✖ Don't forget to bring your own knife and spoon.

✖ Don't drink the water! It will only make you sick. Drink ale, beer, or wine.

STATE OF THE ART KITCHEN

Hurry! Sale ends soon!

Modern kitchens

• Henry VIII's kitchens at Hampton Court are state-of-the-art. They have 50 rooms and measure an amazing 36,000 square feet (3,345 sq m).

• Diners there drink 600 barrels of alcohol a year.

• Roast beef takes nine hours to cook. The spit has to be kept turning all the time the meat is roasting.

• Strict laws say who can sit where—and how much food they can be served.

FASHION, FOLLIES, & FARTHINGALES

The Tudor catwalk was the royal court. The ladies dressed to impress—and Henry was often very impressed indeed. It was different with Elizabeth. She liked to be the center of attention and nobody was allowed to outshine her.

WHAT'S REALLY IN FOR A GIRLS' NIGHT OUT?

Ruffles
Lacy ruffs around the neck, to frame the face!

Pearls
Pearls—in your ears, on your bodice, on your headdress, or those elegant gloves

Big Skirt
Big skirts, stiff and fitted around hoops called farthingales. These are made of willow or whalebone.

Fabric
Make the most of gorgeous fabrics with a "slash" that reveals the satins and silks.

A TIGHT FIT

Do you want really tight sleeves—the height of fashion? Make them detachable, so that they are pinned on or even sewn on each time you wear that dress. Too much hard work? Your maidservants can unpick them for you afterward.

Washing, did you say?

Most people in Tudor times are quite content to wash once every three months, or even less often. After all, who needs to wash when there is perfectly good musk and civet perfume to be purchased down at Cheapside? Queen Elizabeth, on the other hand, likes a hot tub, or so the story goes.

HOT ROCKS

Tudor courtiers, both men and women, wear heaps of fabulously expensive jewelry. Fashions from continental Europe are much in vogue—gleaming pearls, rich gold, cool silver, fiery rubies, or green emeralds from the New World. Elaborate pendants hang from gold chains or silk ribbons. Broaches, or pins, are worn on hats or clothes.

Fancy Threads

Tudor men are as much fashion victims as the women, with their ruffs, doublets and hose, richly embroidered cloth, and fancy earrings. Of course, that is only if you are a courtier. You will wear a less decorative suit if you are a merchant or a businessman. And smelly old rags if you are a beggar—but hey ho, that's life.

Don't Let On!

Sneak a look inside Queen Elizabeth's private chambers! She has 1,000 dresses! And over 80 wigs and hairpieces!

Makeup tips

• Perfumes, creams, and oils are just so necessary for your skin. Some are made from beeswax.

• Use cinnabar, madder, or cochineal for lips and cheeks, henna for nails and hair.

•Want a pale face or need to cover smallpox scars? Got wrinkles or pimples to hide? Lay the white makeup on thick! Watch out—this makeup is made of poisonous lead.

THOMAS CROMWELL

Selling Out

Henry VIII wanted to divorce Catherine of Aragon in order to marry Anne Boleyn, who he thought would give him a male heir. He fell out with the Pope over this and, in 1534, declared himself head of the Church in England. He decided to shut down about 850 monasteries, convents, and religious shrines. He was broke and the monks had fabulous treasures and huge estates. Henry's chief minister Thomas Cromwell seized the churches' riches for the royal coffers.

ABBEYS AT SLASHED PRICES!

HURRY WHILE STOCKS LAST!!

SOMERSET

GLASTONBURY ABBEY, SOMERSET
One of the most famous monasteries in the land, founded in the 600s. Renowned in myth and legend. Abbot recently executed for not cooperating.

YORKSHIRE

FOUNTAINS ABBEY, YORKSHIRE
New on the market, handed over by an abbot in return for an annual pension. Just perfect for property development. A real bargain.

AMAZING DEALS TO BE HAD—ESPECIALLY IF YOU ARE A PAL OF HENRY VIII OR THOMAS CROMWELL

By appointment of
HIS ROYAL HIGHNESS HENRY VIII

Clearance sale of extensive properties and assets formerly in the possession of the Roman Catholic Church

HOW THE SCAM WORKS

1 Send in the commissioners, who accuse the monks of wrong-doing.
2 Seize all money, treasure, books, and precious furnishings.
3 Sell off the land to supporters of the king and friends of Thomas Cromwell in return for loyalty.
4 Knock down buildings and sell materials to local people, and rent out parcels of land.
5 Spend the proceeds on new wars!

HAIL! met up with one of the monks packing his bags. How did he feel?

Between you and me, the abbot did drink a bit too much and some of the monks were up to no good. But that Thomas Cromwell pretends to be Mr. Morality, but the only thing that makes him tick is power. Without any monks and nuns, who will look after the poor and sick?

Head's off

OK, Thomas Cromwell was not really a real estate agent. But he was the wheeler-dealer who got this scam going. He made big bucks and was created Earl of Essex. But he got on the wrong side of Henry VIII over the disastrous marriage deal with Anne of Cleves and had his head cut off (then boiled and stuck on a spike). That was in July 1540.

NORTH IN REVOLT

YORK, 1536

They are calling it "the Pilgrimage of Grace." Across northern England, Catholics have had enough of the king's tyrannical behavior. In York, 9,000 protesters (the king's men claim fewer) have all but taken over the city. Hopes are high that Henry will make his peace with the rebels.

York Minster

LONDON, 1537

Despite the deal he made with the rebels, Henry has decided to impose martial law on the north and execute 216 of them anyway, including nobles, abbots, and monks. Now, there's a surprise!

LAW & ORDER

The law courts of the Tudors were actually pretty fair. But the sentences were severe. In Elizabeth's reign, new laws made things a bit easier for the poor, and that helped cut crime. But on the streets of London there were still spies, secret agents, muggers, and murderers.

VAGABOND!

Why do I wander from town to town? Because I used to graze my cows on land for public use, but they fenced it all off, so I had no work, and I couldn't pay rent. I used to go up to the monastery where they'd give me a bit of work, or some bread and salted herring. Then they shut down the monastery. Now I get whipped from town to town. The king has got a lot to answer for!

I WORK FOR FOOD!

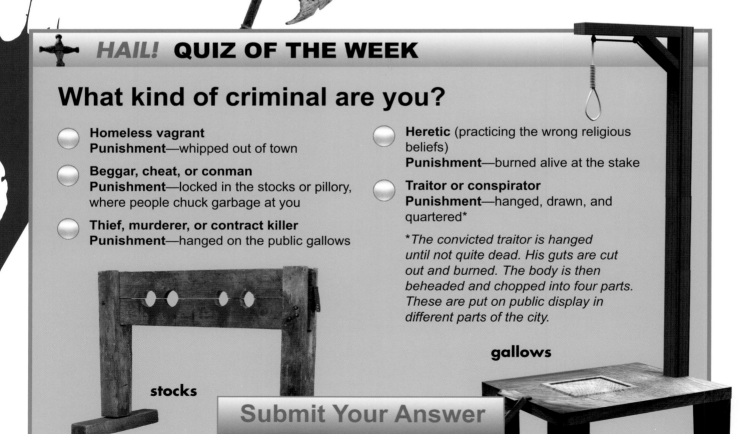

HAIL! QUIZ OF THE WEEK

What kind of criminal are you?

- **Homeless vagrant**
  Punishment—whipped out of town

- **Beggar, cheat, or conman**
  Punishment—locked in the stocks or pillory, where people chuck garbage at you

- **Thief, murderer, or contract killer**
  Punishment—hanged on the public gallows

- **Heretic** (practicing the wrong religious beliefs)
  Punishment—burned alive at the stake

- **Traitor or conspirator**
  Punishment—hanged, drawn, and quartered*

*The convicted traitor is hanged until not quite dead. His guts are cut out and burned. The body is then beheaded and chopped into four parts. These are put on public display in different parts of the city.

gallows

stocks

Submit Your Answer

Some of the language on the streets of London is called "cant," a secret lingo known only to the criminal underworld. Here are some of the words they use:

angler A thief who uses a hooked pole to steal items through open windows

bawdy-basket A door-to-door seller who befriends servants in order to steal

coney-catcher A conman who swindles you out of your money

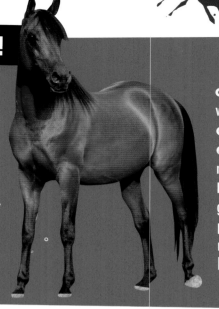

counterfeit crank A beggar who pretends to be an invalid

cutpurse A mugger, a robber

dell Homeless woman or runaway maidservant, living off crime

kinchin mort A baby or young girl used for begging and stealing

prigger A horse thief

ruffler A fancy-dressing villain or bully, often an old soldier

Keeping watch

HAIL! comes across a guardian of the peace on his nightly round.

"TWELVE OF THE CLOCK, LOOK WELL TO YOUR LOCKS!"

Q *"Excuse me, officer, why are you yelling and ringing your bell at midnight?"*

A "To let evildoers know that the forces of law and order are on patrol."

Q *"What's your job, exactly?"*

A "Parish constable, member of the Watch for the last five years. I don't catch many villains, but my dog puts the fear of the Lord in 'em!"

SPYMASTER "W"

Sir Francis Walsingham is a gray, shadowy figure, a genius at sniffing out treason and plots against Queen Elizabeth. He has secret agents everywhere, in England and across Europe. Watch out, you traitors!

GRISLY STABBING IN DEPTFORD

Famous playwright Kit Marlowe killed in drunken brawl!

LONDON, 30 May 1593

London was awash with rumors today after the death of top drama writer Christopher Marlowe in a tavern. His murderers were said to be members of an underworld gang. Do they have links with the Secret Service? Was Marlowe really an agent himself? Was he really a dangerous atheist? Was he just drunk? And were his plays any good? We demand to know whether there has been a cover-up!

WELCOME TO MY
BEAUTIFUL HOME!

We go inside a choice selection of Tudor homes to admire the decor, furnishings, and location. How would you give them a makeover?

Estate-of-the-art

No more drafty old castles for the royals. This is the age of luxury palaces, with big fireplaces and tall chimneys. The ultimate new residence has to be Nonesuch Palace, near Epsom in Surrey (right). They say it cost Henry VIII a veritable fortune, so only suitable for the Tudor billionaire!

LOCATION, LOCATION

Hardwick Hall, Derbyshire ▶

Hilltop site. Built for the Countess of Shrewsbury in the 1590s. Huge windows to let in the light and show how much money she spent on glass.

▲ Newlands Farm, Stratford-upon-Avon

Later known as Anne Hathaway's Cottage, this was the childhood home of William Shakespeare's wife. That rural look includes a cute thatched roof and timbering, and there is a lovely cottage garden.

◀ Plas Mawr, Conwy, Wales

This fine townhouse was built in 1577–85 for a wealthy Welsh gent called Robert Wynn. Urban setting with brewhouse, kitchens, and pantry.

Interior Design

Oak paneling? Flemish tapestry? Decorated ceilings? Show just how stylish you can be.

• A quiet word of advice: a few Tudor rose logos (below right) help to show whose side you are on.

• That polished oak look is a classic, and will really last. Show off the finest carving on chests and cupboards, benches, stools—and thrones (top right).

• Four-poster beds (left) keep out the draft and are very cosy and comfy. But the finishing touch is the chic fabric chosen for the drapes and bedcovers.

The garden scene

❀ In vogue for Tudor garden designs are intricate "knot" patterns of low hedges (above) and gravel paths. You could add a maze as a fun puzzle for your guests, or fountain to tinkle away on a summer's day.

❀ Border the paths with fragrant shrubs such as rosemary and lavender. These can be strewn on the floors of the house to keep it smelling sweet.

❀ Scented flowers can make sweet bouquets or nosegays to keep away the plague. And all sorts of medicinal plants, such as rhubarb, can sort out a bad tummy or headache.

Beware those smells!

If you are a royal, then it is best to move from one palace to another through the seasons. The toilets do get rather smelly, and the palaces can be given a good clean-out while you are gone.

There are no proper sewers or drains. If you own a townhouse, then you'll be well aware of the odor that hits you on the rat-infested streets every day. And foul smells bring diseases with them.

BEHIND THE SCENES

HAIL!'s reporters go behind the scenes at a big country house

Q *So you are a maidservant here? You must be proud to work in such a lovely house.*

A I don't know about that. I'm certainly exhausted! All those stairs! All that water to carry from the well in the yard!

Q *Do they treat you well?*

A Lady P. is alright, but that daughter's stuck-up!

Q *What are you up to now?*

A Carrying a warming pan up to my lady's bedroom. Must dash.

Warming pan

What's On in TUDOR TOWN?

Cockfight

Traditional Shrove Tuesday entertainment. Two one-year-old cockerels fighting—see the feathers fly and place your bets!

Globe Theater, London

Another chance to catch the popular play *Romeo and Juliet* by William Shakespeare. A real heartbreaker!

Grand Ball At The Royal Court

Fashion heaven! Strictly for courtiers, though, or foreign ambassadors. You might just catch glimpses of their carriages as you wait in the wind and the rain. And inside the palace (left), there is such dancing and merriment!

London Bear-Garden And Bull Ring Theater

See the mastiffs go in and bait the bulls and bears! Watch as big sums of money are won or lost! Even Queen Elizabeth has been known to drop by to watch the blood flow.

Mayday Revels

Anywhere in the kingdom on May 1 you will find houses decked in greenery, the May Queen and Jack o'Green, drums, and dancing. See St. George fight the Dragon! Watch amazing amounts of ale flow!

Midsummer Bonfires

Ring in Midsummer's Eve with bells, bonfires, and pageants. Keep clear of the pious—they might object!

HAIL!'s Party People team is here to help you find out what is going on. Are you visiting London or are you traveling around the country? Wherever you go, there are always a lot of laughs to be had. And cultural feasts can be found in the most unlikely places!

All the world's a stage

There is a new play on the London stage that is sure to become a smash hit. The writer is Master Will Shakespeare, who has taken the capital by storm in recent years. *The Tragedy of Hamlet, Prince of Denmark* has it all—a murder, a ghost, madness, love, and a play within a play. At the end, the corpses are piled high! Even the groundlings, the mob in the open yard at the front of the stage, fell silent. Actor Richard Burbage masters his leading role.

RATING ★☆☆☆

QUEEN LAUGHS HERSELF TO BITS!

Queen Elizabeth I admitted last night that she is the number 1 fan of Shoreditch-based comic Richard Tarlton, everyone's favorite stand-up (or fall-down)! It is a well-known fact that all players are rogues, but few players are like our Richard. He has made his name by taking on hecklers and winning. He is a brilliant clown who makes up witty improv songs.

RATING
★★★☆

STOP PRESS
LONDON, June 12 1599

This evening sees the opening night at the Globe Theater (left), built by the Lord Chamberlain's Men, the actors company who are shareholders in this enterprise. Richard Burbage and his brother Cuthbert own 25 percent each, while William Shakespeare (the playwright of the company) and three others own 12.5 percent each. They have built the theater on some marshy gardens in Southwark, south London.

YOUR LETTERS

**Got a problem? Share it with our readers!
Our WISE WOMAN offers the best advice.**

*Dear Wise Woman,
I just don't seem to be able to hold
down a relationship. I am now
on my sixth wife. I'm a good catch.
You'd have thought I would have
found Mistress Right by now.*

Henry R, Hampton Court

Dear Henry R,
Hasn't it ever occurred to you that it's you
who might be Master Wrong? Tidy yourself
up! Perhaps you're the sort of person who
chops off people's heads. Don't, if you want
a friend as well as a wife!

Dear Wise Woman,
My son, William, is as lazy as they come.
His first Latin class at school doesn't
start until the very reasonable hour of
seven in the morning, but can I get him
out of bed? He creeps like a snail to school,
most unwillingly.

Stratford-upon-Avon

*Dear Wise Woman,
I rule a kingdom, but I
only have the body of a
weak and feeble woman.
My Spanish brother-in-
law is sending a war fleet
or Armada to invade my
country. What can I do?*

Elizabeth R, Greenwich

Dear Mistress S,
I blame the teachers. Your son is obviously not
being beaten enough with those birch twigs!
If you spare the rod, you will spoil the child.

Dear Elizabeth R,
Your brother-in-law sounds like a
real bully. Why don't you call all
your soldiers and sailors together
and tell them that you have the
heart and stomach of a king.
I am sure they'll all cheer and
send him and his so-called
Armada packing. Atta girl!

Dear Wise Woman,

I'm Queen of Scots, and when I got chucked out of Scotland, I thought I'd go and stay with my cousin Bess, who's Queen of England. OK, she's a Protestant and I'm a Catholic, but I did expect some hospitality, since we're family. I got hospitality alright—at Her Majesty's pleasure. Imprisoned for 19 years! Life is SO unfair!

MM'CR

Mary Stuart, Fotheringhay Castle

WISE WOMAN WRITES:

Sadly, since this letter appeared in our column, Mary, Queen of Scots has been executed. We extend our sympathy to her family and friends—and her poor little dog.

Dear Mary, Queen of Scots,

You have every right to be angry. What are families like these days? Now don't lose your head, it might never happen. On the other hand, it might, so you'd better start saying your prayers.

Is it Really All in the Stars?

The queen's personal astrologer, Dr. John Dee, looks into his crystal ball for *HAIL!*

I welcome this chance to have a chat with the readers of *HAIL!*. As you know I am a mathematician and scientist with a long beard, so I do live in the real world. I can confirm indeed that the stars and planets have an influence on our daily lives. It is as obvious as the fact that metals of no value can be turned into solid gold. We can predict the future, and speak with angels and the spirits of the dead.

TRAVEL SUPPLEMENT

The Tudor era was the age of exploration, particularly by sea. New worlds awaited adventurous travelers. We look at some of those brave souls who set sail for far-flung, and often dangerous, lands.

GO FOR GOLD!

Sir Martin Frobisher took off on a trip to China, but instead went to Canada—three times!! He brought back tons of "gold," but it was actually worthless iron pyrites—"fool's gold."

Tip: Travelers need to do their homework properly.

Beware unseen dangers

Sir Francis Drake sailed round the entire world. He got rich, he saw amazing sights, and managed to dodge both the cannonballs and the cannibals. But he did get a terrible stomach bug on a trip to Panama, and sadly it finished him off!

Tip: Don't drink the local water.

WIN YOUR OWN GLOBE

Just like the queen's! But there are still a few bits that are blank, as there are so many places to explore.

Eldorado no-show

Walter Raleigh was the man who, in 1584, began a colony at Virginia, in North America, naming it after "the Virgin Queen," Elizabeth I. He went to South America and heard these rumors about a fabulous place called Eldorado. He wrote all about it, and later, James I sent Walter off to find it. But it did not exist! Heads rolled, alas.

Tip: Don't believe all the travel books!

Wonders of the world

The great thing about Tudor seafarers whizzing around the world is that they can tell us about the lands they have seen and whether all those old medieval travelers' tales were really true or just myths.

HAIL! can now absolutely confirm that unicorns, dragons, and mermaids exist—the evidence comes from sailors who have seen them! We just cannot wait to see these amazing sights with our own eyes.

PIRATE FORECAST

Do you fancy a sunny Mediterranean cruise or a fishing trip closer to home? Never leave on vacation without checking our pirate forecast, or you may end up as a galley slave!

- **North African Coast**—Fierce activity by Barbary corsairs in search of Christian slaves and treasure

- **West Coast of Ireland**—Grainne ni Mhaille (we call her Grace O'Malley) has been running a pirate fleet out of Clew Bay, but the rumor is she's ready to do a peace deal with Queen Elizabeth herself.

- **North Sea**—Things are more peaceful since Klein Hänslein and 33 other pirates were beheaded in Hamburg in 1573.

Psst! Do readers remember Thomas Stukeley, accused of piracy in 1558? The one who later rebelled against Queen Elizabeth? Well, people say his father might have been Henry VIII himself! A real Tudor pirate...

HAIL!'S TRIBUTE TO THE PASSING OF AN AGE

118 GLORIOUS YEARS

Sad to say, the age of the Tudors has come to an end. In this issue, we commemorate the reign of Queen Elizabeth I and mark the end of the Tudor dynasty.

March 24, 1603
For some months, the Queen has been in poor health and really not looking herself at all. We must now report that in the early hours of this morning, Elizabeth I passed away peacefully at Richmond Palace at the age of 69.

What a send-off!

You should have seen the funeral of Elizabeth I. The horses were draped in black velvet, the banners with the royal coats-of-arms held high, and every great noble in the land in the procession to Westminster Abbey (below). Crowds packed the streets and rooftops to see the passing of an age.

Did you know?

On the top of the coffin was a full-sized model of the queen, made of wax. It was dressed in the queen's richest robes. A crown was placed on the model's head and a scepter in its hand.

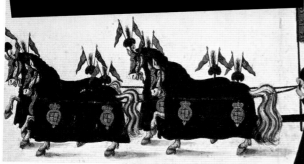

WHO WILL INHERIT?

That is the question that has been on everyone's lips for months. Elizabeth had no husband—despite all her suitors—so no children to inherit the throne. We all fear for our future.

UNDER NEW MANAGEMENT

The Stuarts were the royal family of Scotland. They were related by marriage to the Tudors and became the next rulers of England and Wales. A horseman galloped from London to Scotland in just three days to carry the news to the future James I.

Meet the Stuarts

King James VI of Scotland will be known as James I south of the border, becoming king of both countries. This is an amazing turn of events, because it was his mother, Mary, Queen of Scots, who was executed by Queen Elizabeth back in 1587.

Did you know?

King James is a bit of a campaigner. He has a thing about witches and also about that newfangled weed, tobacco. He does not approve of either!

LOOKING BACK

How did people remember the Tudor age? At the time, people did not like the Tudors much, and even Elizabeth was not popular in her old age.

But the Stuarts were so incredibly stuck-up and bossy that in the end the people decided to cut off a king's head! In 1649, they executed Charles I. By then, people were recalling Tudor times as the "good old days of jollity, roast beef, and Good Queen Bess." That's nostalgia for you!

Charles I

HAIL! has found some old fogies who still remember the Tudors.

"I tell you what, it was more peaceful in England and Wales in those days. There were wars in other places of course, but I never had to fight.

"Tudors? Stuarts? They're all the same if you ask me. We poor folk still have to plow the fields, and the roof of our cottage still leaks.

"Oh my grandfather did frightfully well back in the days of Henry VIII. We made our fortune, and we are still rich today."

GLOSSARY

adultery To have an affair while still married

annulment To end a marriage beause it is invalid according to the Church

armada A large fleet of warships

cinnabar A red mineral used as a cosmetic

civet An animal whose strong scent is used in the making of perfumes

cochineal A natural red dye made from insects and exported to Europe from the New World

coffers treasury

courtier A servant or attendant in a royal court

doublet A close-fitting jacket worn by men

dynasty Rulers from the same family line

exiled Forced by law to leave one's home or country

Flemish Describing someone from Flanders, a region crossing France, Belgium, and the Nertherlands

henna A natural reddish brown dye from a plant

Lent A period of fasting and repentence

madder A natural reddish pink dye from a plant

martial law Military rule by a state over its citizens in times of emergency

mastiff A large breed of dog used for guard duty

Middle Ages A period in Europe from about 500 to 1500 CE

Midsummer's Eve A pre-Christian festival held on June 23, marked by bonfires and feasts.

nostalgia A longing for something past

pavilion A large lavish tent

pilgrimage A journey to a shrine or holy place

pillory Public punishment in which a person's head and hands were locked into a wooden frame

plague A deadly infection of the lungs, blood, or lymph nodes; common during the Tudor era

rogue A mischievous person

Shrove Tuesday The last day before the Christian fasting period known as Lent

stocks Public punishment in which a person's feet were locked into a wooden frame for a few hours

tapestry A woven wall hanging, featuring designs or pictures

TB Tuberculosis, a deadly infection of the lungs

tyrannical Behaving like a tyrant; cruel or harsh

virginal A musical instrument with a keyboard

1485 Battle of Bosworth Field; Henry VII becomes the first Tudor king

1520 Field of the Cloth of Gold meeting in France between Henry VIII and François I

1533 Henry VIII marries Anne Boleyn

1547 Edward VI becomes king of England

1450 CE

1525

1545

1509 Henry VIII beomes king and marries his first wife, Catherine of Aragon

1531 Henry VIII becomes head of the Church in England and Wales

1535 Start of the closing down of the Monasteries

ON THE INTERNET

Excellent site covering everything from the *Mary Rose*, Henry VIII's flagship, to daily life and Tudor spies.
www.bbc.co.uk/history/british/tudors/

Original documents about the Spanish Armada and searching questions.
www.nationalarchives.gov.uk/education/lesson39.htm

Comprehensive site including biographies, events, the theater, poverty, and religion
www.spartacus.schoolnet.co.uk/Tudors.htm

Many articles on the major events and big personalities that dominated Tudor history
www.historylearningsite.co.uk/tudor_england.htm

Family trees, photos, timelines, and lists
www.tudorhistory.org/

Food, clothes, sports, exploration, music, and other Tudor topics
www.elizabethan-era.org.uk/

History of the famous London stage, its actors, audiences, and its most famous playwright William Shakespeare
www.globe-theatre.org.uk/

Education, medicine, homes, and other aspects of Tudor social history
www.localhistories.org/tudor.html

BOOKS

A Tudor Journey by Philip Steele(Wayland, 2003)

Britain Through the Ages: Tudors by Felicity Hebditch (Evans Brothers, 2003)

Real Lives: Tudor Children by Sallie Purkiss (A&C Black, 2004)

People in the Past: Tudor Rich and Poor by Haydn Middleton (Heinemann Library, 2004)

Eyewitness: Tudor by Simon Adams(Dorling Kindersley, 2008)

Henry VIII:Royal Beheader by Sean Stewart Price (Franklin Watts, 2009)

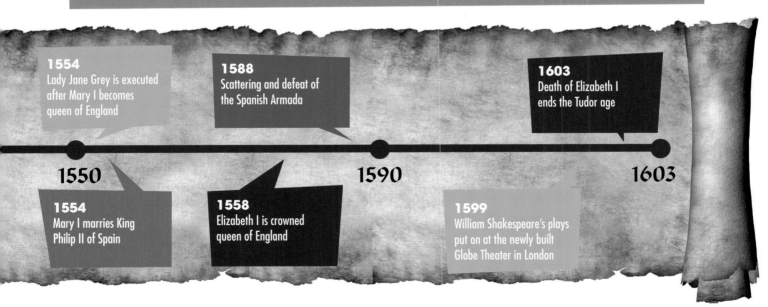

1554 Lady Jane Grey is executed after Mary I becomes queen of England

1588 Scattering and defeat of the Spanish Armada

1603 Death of Elizabeth I ends the Tudor age

1550

1590

1603

1554 Mary I marries King Philip II of Spain

1558 Elizabeth I is crowned queen of England

1599 William Shakespeare's plays put on at the newly built Globe Theater in London

INDEX